John Connolly

A Narrative of the Transactions, Imprisonment, and Sufferings

Of John Connolly, an American Loyalist and Lieutenant-colonel in...

John Connolly

A Narrative of the Transactions, Imprisonment, and Sufferings
Of John Connolly, an American Loyalist and Lieutenant-colonel in...

ISBN/EAN: 9783744758758

Printed in Europe, USA, Canada, Australia, Japan

Cover: Foto ©ninafisch / pixelio.de

More available books at **www.hansebooks.com**

A

NARRATIVE

OF THE

TRANSACTIONS, IMPRISONMENT,

AND

SUFFERINGS,

OF

JOHN CONNOLLY,

AN

AMERICAN LOYALIST,

AND

LIEUTENANT-COLONEL in his Majesty's Service.

IN WHICH ARE SHEWN,

The unjustifiable Proceedings of CONGRESS, in his
TREATMENT and DETENTION.

LONDON:

Printed in the Year MDCCLXXXIII.

A

NARRATIVE

OF THE

TRANSACTIONS, IMPRISONMENT,

AND

SUFFERINGS,

OF

JOHN CONNOLLY,

AN

AMERICAN LOYALIST,

AND

LIEUTENANT-COLONEL in his Majesty's Service,

IN WHICH ARE SHEWN,

The unjustifiable Proceedings of CONGRESS, in his
TREATMENT and DETENTION.

LONDON:

Printed in the Year MDCCLXXXIII.

REPRINTED FOR

CHARLES L. WOODWARD,

NEW YORK, 1889.

A NARRATIVE OF THE TRANSACTIONS, IMPRISONMENT, AND SUFFERINGS OF JOHN CONNOLLY, AN AMERICAN LOYALIST AND LIEUT. COL. IN HIS MAJESTY'S SERVICE.

There cannot, perhaps, be a more severe task imposed upon a person, who has any pretensions to that sense of propriety which distinguishes a delicate mind, than to be obliged to relate a long story, of which he is himself the subject. It has, however, always been held excusable if the incidents were extraordinary, and it were necessary to the future peace and prosperity of the narrator they should be known, provided the tale were told with modesty and truth. I hope this gentle indulgence will be kindly extended to me, and that the unavoidable egotism that must pervade this narrative, will be benevolently overlooked in mercy to the misfortunes of one who is at least conscious of having acted with good intentions, and from principles which he believed were descriptive of a loyal subject, an honest man, and a man of honour.

I was born in America of respectable parents, and received as perfect an education as that country could afford. In the early part of life I was bred to physic, the practice of which it was intended I should pursue; my natural bent of mind, however, determined otherwise. It was my ambition to be a soldier; and this passion was so prevalent that, contrary to the wishes of my friends, I went a volunteer, while yet a youth, to Martinico, where I endeavoured to distinguish myself, as far as inexperience and an unimportant station would admit. After the peace of 1762, the North American Indians entered into a general confederacy to destroy our frontier settlements and demolish the garrisons. The British commander in chief was obliged to send an army to repel these invaders; in which, once more a

1

volunteer, I served two campaigns, at my own private expense; and, as became me, cheerfully and ambitiously encountered the dangers and fatigues of war. Here I had an opportunity of observing the great difference between the *petite guerre* of the Indians, and the military system of the Europeans, and how essentially necessary it was for a good soldier in this service to be master of them both. Animated by a strong desire to make myself worthy to serve my King and country on future occasions, after peace was established with the Indians, I explored our newly acquired territory, visited the various tribes of native Americans, studied their different manners and customs, undertook the most toilsome marches with them through the extensive wilds of Canada, and depended upon the precarious chace for my subsistence for months successively. A perseverance in these preliminary duties of a good soldier taught me to endure hardships, and gave me agility of body, and an aptitude to enterprize, very proper to form a partizan officer.

Delighted with the soil and climate, I afterwards fixed my residence beyond the Apalachian mountains in West Augusta county, and as numbers were daily emigrating thither from the middle Colonies, I was active in encouraging the new settlers; these soon acquired property, the spirit of industry increased, cultivation and improvements were extended, and establishments, scarcely credible, arose from the midst of a wilderness, and spread for more than one hundred miles down the river Ohio. To be at the head of a new settlement was not the only object I had in view. During the preceding war, France had sent her soldiers from Canada, and by seizing this country, and erecting Fort Du Quesne (now Fort Pitt) had given great disturbance to Virginia, and the Middle Colonies in general. This new settlement precluded the possibility of renewing the like ravages from Louisiana, now the only avenue through which we were vulnerable, in case of future hostilities with the House of Bourbon. I had been taught from my earliest infancy to revere my King and country, and provide against their enemies: I had here an opportunity of performing my duty, and I was happy.

In the infancy of the settlement, the magistrates of Pennsylvania usurped a power of jurisdiction that was not only illegal but extremely prejudicial to the inhabitants; to preserve which, they proceeded to many very unjustifiable acts of violence. and went even so far as to threaten an appeal to the sword. I was the person, who having the most power, had the greatest share in procuring a redress of these grievances. I was sensible the Charter limits of the Province of Pennsylvania could not justify the exercise of jurisdiction beyond the Western bounds of that government; and therefore applied to the Governor and Council of Virginia, and obtained the necessary authority to prohibit such usurpation, until his Majesty's royal pleasure was known. These things are mentioned, not to display my own merits or consequences, but because they are necessary to the narrative; for though it was my endeavour, throughout this transaction, to conduct myself with a dispassionate and candid regard to justice only, yet, as it was prejudicial to the pecuniary interests of some individuals in Pennsylvania, they became my enemies, among whom, was a Gentleman since advanced to high military rank in the American service.

In the year 1774, disputes arose between the Indians and some inconsiderate people, who, it appeared from every circumstance, had treated the former in a very harsh and improper manner; reciprocal injuries took place, and the industrious and meritorious husbandman, with his innocent family, suffered for the injustice committed by his unprincipled countrymen. I was, at that time, invested with the command of the militia; it was, therefore, my peculiar duty to avert, if possible, a war that threatened the destruction of a flourishing Colony, and every endeavour at pacification was employed by me, but unhappily without effect. Depredations continued, and the defenceless inhabitants fled from the vengeance of their enraged enemies. However, in obedience to the orders of his excellency Lord Dunmore, I raised a body of men sufficient to cover the frontier, and by a chain of small forts repelled the violence of their incursions. Hostilities did not end here; other Indian nations joined the confederacy, and the war became more important. Two small armies were marched into the enemies' country, as the sole means of effecting a speedy and permanent reconciliation. Lord Dunmore, in person, commanded, and a battle, the most important that ever happened on a similar occasion, in North America, was fought, in which the Indians were totally routed, pursued to their towns, and reduced to the necessity of giving hostages for the accomplishment of a treaty of peace entered into by them, and which was to have been finally ratified the ensuing Spring at Pittsburgh. I cannot speak in terms sufficiently expressive of the admiration with which the whole army beheld Lord Dunmore, during this expedition. His conduct was exemplary to the officer and the soldier: he chearfully encountered every hardship, waded through every creek, and marched with his men upwards of Four hundred miles on foot. He preserved the dignity, by fulfilling the duties of his station.

In the course of the contest, the principal warriors and chiefs were made prisoners, and committed to my charge at Fort Pitt, where, after the expedition, I had the honour to command some Colony troops as Major Commandant. I have before spoken of the efforts I had used to qualify myself for the profession of arms; and I had now the satisfaction to meet every honourable testimony of applause for my behaviour in the Indian war, both from his excellency Lord Dunmore and my fellow-subjects.

Although Congress had assembled themselves in September 1774, yet as that was about the time I was going into the Indian country, my mind was so intent upon the war, I paid but little regard to political heats which every loyalist imagined would soon subside; but on my return, the intimations of my friends, and the proceedings of the disaffected, gave me the first unhappy presages of the ensuing commotions. These were greatly heightened by the following letter, which I received from General Washington, in answer to one I had written to him on Indian affairs.

MOUNT-VERNON, Feb. 25, 1775.

DEAR SIR,

Your servant, on his return from Williamsburg, affords me occasion to answer your polite letter. I confess the state of affairs is sufficiently alarming; which our critical situation, with regard to the Indians does not diminish: but as you have wrote to Lord Dunmore, relative to the prisoners under your charge, there can be no doubt of his Lordship's having now transmitted you the necessary directions on that subject. I have only to express my most ardent wishes that every measure, consistent with reason and sound policy, may be adopted to keep those people, at this time, in good humour; for another rupture would not only ruin the external, but internal parts of this government. If the journal of your proceedings in the Indian war is to be published, I shall have an opportunity of seeing what I have long coveted. With us here, things wear a disagreeable aspect; and the minds of men are exceedingly disturbed at the measures of the British government. The King's Speech and Address of both Houses, prognosticate nothing favourable to us; but by some subsequent proceedings thereto, *as well as by private letters from London,* there is reason to believe, the Ministry would willingly change their ground, from a conviction the forcible measures will be inadequate to the end designed. A little time must now unfold the mystery, as matters are drawing to a point.

I am, dear sir,
your friend, and most obedient
humble servant,
G. WASHINGTON.

MAJOR CONNOLLY,
Fort Pitt.

This letter spoke in plain terms the spirit of its dictator, and the intelligence I received from all quarters confirmed my apprehensions. And here I have the consolation to

reflect, that my loyalty to my Prince, and respect for the
established form of government, were too confirmed to
admit of the least doubt which party I should espouse; I
decided instantly, and resolved to exert every faculty in
defence of the royal cause; from which resolution not one
idea has ever swerved, although my succeeding misfortunes left me only the inclination, while it deprived me of
the power to execute. At this time, indeed, I had better
prospects; for notwithstanding that those illegal assemblies,
called county committees, had generally pervaded the thir-
teen Provinces, I had influence enough, not only to prevent
any such a͏ ᷄ly in West Augusta county, where I presided, but ͏ ᷄ to engage a formidable body of friends,
at the risk ᷄ and fortune, in support of the constitutional authority.

The battle of Bunker's Hill had now been fought, and
the flames of rebellion began openly to blaze. I had written
to Lord Dunmore for instructions respecting my conduct,
who, I found, would be obliged to quit his government; and
received for answer, that he advised me to disband the
troops, at the time limited by act of assembly, that they
might have no cause of complaint on that head; that I
should convene the Indians to a general treaty, restore the
prisoners, and endeavour to incline them to espouse the
royal cause. This last proved a most hazardous enterprize,
though not therefore relinquished; for the assembly of
Virginia, having resolved themselves into an unwarrantable
convention, finding I had invited the contiguous Indian
tribes to a general congress at Fort Pitt, deputed a committee of their own body to inspect my conduct. These people
were ordered to impress upon the minds of the Indians, the
justice of the hostile proceedings against this country, and
the necessity of arming as a preliminary to the intended
requisition of their auxiliary aid in future. This was the
direct contrary to what it was my duty, if possible, to effect;
and, narrowly as I was watched, I had the happiness to
succeed in this dangerous and critical undertaking.

This was owing to my superior knowledge of Indian

manners and tempers, and the measures I had previously taken. I had most assiduously cultivated the friendship, and insinuated myself into the favour of my prisoners; had convinced them of the advantages that might accrue to their nations, by adhering to the British government; and procured their promises to negotiate the business with their brethren, which they punctually performed. Thus I secretly frustrated the machinations of the Republicans, while I received their thanks, and procured assurances from the Indian chiefs to support his Majesty, at all events, as his Majesty's most faithful friends and auxilliaries; as a proof of which, I was authorized to transmit a large belt of wampum to Lord Dunmore, from him to be sent to his Majesty, as a symbol of their inviolable attachment to his royal person. This public transaction employed a fortnight, at the end of which I dismissed the Indians perfectly satisfied and informed; having first added an additional and considerable present out of my private fortune, to what had been publicly voted for that purpose.

The troops lately under my command were now disbanded, the demagogues of faction were active, the spirit of sedition was every where prevalent, and distrust of each other pervaded hearts the most loyal. But as nothing great or good could be effected in times like these without risk, I considered only what plan was best at such conjuncture; and having determined, resolved to act with vigor, as a temporizing neutrality was neither consistent with my principles nor my passions. My design briefly was, first to engage as many gentlemen of consequence as possible to join with me in defence of government, and afterwards to make my way through the country, visit Lord Dunmore, who was now driven, for personal safety, on board a ship lying at Norfolk, consult with him, and take his instructions concerning the most effectual mode I and my adherents could pursue to serve his Majesty. I began by inviting such of my friends as I could best depend on to an entertainment, where, as public disturbances were now the universal topic, little address was necessary

to introduce such discourse. Encouraged by an unanimity
of opinion, each man delivered his sentiments freely; and
as I found them universally enraged against the arbitrary
proceedings of the Republican party, I ventured to predict,
that nothing less than independency, and a total revolution,
were intended by the leaders of faction, whatever might be
their pretentions. My friends were men warmed with a high
veneration for his Majesty, and the constitution; and as the
conversation operated as I could wish, I found means to
take some of the most confidential aside, and inform them
of my plan, of my resolution to execute it at the hazard of
life and fortune, and of my expectation of their hearty concurrence and aid. The gentlemen present were most of
them either officers in the militia, or magistrates of the
county, consequently were those whose influence and wealth
could most effectually serve the cause. A solemn compact
was immediately entered into, stating, that if an accommo-
dation did not take place, and I could procure the necessary
authority to raise men, they would, at the risk of life and
property, most willingly engage to restore the constitutional
authority, as far as any co-operative measure from that
county could contribute to so salutary a design, after which
the strictest secrecy was enjoined, and the company separated.

The circumspection and art necessary to escape to Lord
Dunmore, occasioned some preparatory delay; and the
following incident, which will give a lively picture of the
anarchy of the times, made this delay still greater. Two
nights before my intended departure, my servant entered
my room after midnight, to inform me that an express was
just arrived, with dispatches from Lord Dunmore, and desired admittance. I ordered him to be brought in, and immediately a man followed my servant in a travelling dress,
with a packet in his hand. I drew my curtain, received it,
and was breaking open the seal, when the villain seized me
by the throat, presented a pistol at my breast, told me I was
his prisoner, and, if I offered the least resistance, a dead
man. I had been so long learning to despise danger, and
acquire fortitude, that I was not easily to be intimidated.

I rightly suspected he had accomplices, so leaping up, I drove the fellow back, seized him, and while struggling gave the door a kick, and shut it by the spring-lock. I called to my servant for my sword or pistols; but to his stupefaction, it is probable, I owe my present existence; for though I should have killed my antagonist in self-defence, I should have fallen the immediate martyr of revenge. My door was quickly burst open by his armed coadjutors, about twenty in number; and the contest becoming unequal, I was compelled to submit myself their prisoner. I was scarcely allowed time to dress, my servants were secured; I was mounted on a horse brought for the purpose, hurried away, and obliged to ride all night at the risk of my neck, till about ten o'clock in the morning, when I found myself at Ligonier, fifty-four miles from Pittsburgh.

I soon learnt I was in the power of my inveterate enemy, the commander of the militia, and principal man of the place; who had taken this opportunity of wreaking his malice, under pretence of seizing a dangerous person and a Tory, an appellation lately revived, and given by the republicans to the loyalists; and which the common people were taught to hold in such abhorrence, that Tory was, in their imaginations, synonimous to every thing vile and wicked. My only hope, and that a very distant one, was, a rescue by my friends; and as I was informed, that I was suspected of an intention to raise a body of men to act against the liberties of America, to answer which accusation I must immediately be sent to Congress, I found I could only escape, by gaining time, and protracting a journey so destructive to all my future designs. The agitation of mind unavoidable in such times, and under such circumstances, with the fatigue of such a jaunt, had brought on a slight indisposition, which I purposely magnified, and prevailed on the gentleman in whose custody I was, to suffer me to go to bed; where by continuing the same pretence, I remained all day, and when night came was indulged with a farther respite till the next morning. My wish was, that my friends, who had the cause of royalty as well as friendship at heart, would gain the passes of the Lawrel-hill [Laurel-Hills] or Allegheny mountains, and there effect my rescue.

In the morning, when we had breakfasted, the guard had mounted, and I reluctantly on the point of setting out for Philadelphia, a man on horseback arrived at Ligonier from the mountains, who had apparently rode very hard. He was stopped by the Captain of the guard, and I soon perceived, by their whispers and change of countenance, he brought intelligence they did not like; and almost at the same instant, another person was seen coming, with the greatest expedition, in the contrary direction from Pittsburgh, whom I soon knew to be one of my neighbours, though not perfectly satisfied at that time of his loyalty. To me these were favourable omens, and my conjectures were quickly confirmed, by the arrival of the Gentleman who planned and directed this expedition, and who now saluted me very civilly, entered into conversation, spoke of the disagreeable prospect of civil war, and the unjustifiable attempts of the British legislature; which supposition I repelled, as far as the delicacy of my situation would permit.

Happening to pass through the kitchen of the public house where we were, one of the maids followed me out, and informed me, that a considerable body of my friends were waiting at the Lawrel-hill, who had vowed to put every man to the sword whom they should find guarding me, and afterwards to burn down the house of the principal, in reveng' for such a lawless outrage. This intelligence perfectly explained appearances, and gave me boldness, so that when I re-entered, I presently came to an eclaircissement with my enemy. I observed to him, that his conduct seemed to precipitate the horrors of civil dissention, and that his having recourse to an armed force to remove me out of my own country, in so hostile and suspicious a manner, could not fail to awaken the resentment of my friends, who, undoubtedly, on such a pressing occasion, would have recourse to force also, and repel violence by violence: I added, that it was mutually our duty to suppress, not encourage such proceedings, for they were indubitably big with the most dreadful calamities. The conclusion was, I was permitted to return home, and very gladly took my leave. I had not yet, however, passed the boundaries of danger.—

I had not proceeded far on my return, before I met one of my servants with a led horse, and a portmanteau of cloaths for my use, in case I had been taken to Philadelphia. He informed me of several persons he had seen assembled at Hannah's Town, whose political characters were the reverse of mine, and that he suspected they intended me some injury; and accordingly we presently saw three persons approach, whom I knew to be Magistrates of Pennsylvania, and whom I had some time before been under the necessity of arresting and holding to bail, because they would persist to execute their magisterial functions beyond the limits of their own province and county, (as related in the beginning of this narrative), very much to the prejudice of his Majesty's subjects in the colony of Virginia. These Gentlemen, who were accompanied by the Sheriff, after a hasty salute, arrested me on a writ of twenty thousand pounds damages, for having confined their persons. They proposed returning to Ligonier with me ; to this I objected, alledging, that the action was of so strange a nature, I would not give bail, but insisted on being taken to the county gaol, which was near my own home and friends.

My partizans having heard of my release at Ligonier, and not suspecting any farther attempts, were satisfied and dispersed, and remained quiet two or three days; but when they heard I was again detained at Hannah's Town, under a fresh pretext, they were greatly enraged, and were only prevented from proceeding to extremities, by the prudence of a few individuals. A letter was, however, immediately sent from the senior Magistrate of the county, over which I had the honor to preside, to the committee of Westmoreland county, written in a firm but proper tone, demanding my release. This had instantly the desired effect, and I was at length allowed to return to Pittsburg, where I was met by a great number of my adherents, armed, and impatiently waiting the issue. My gra⸱ ⸱e and feelings at the firmness of their attachment were powerful, and after returning them my thanks in the most expressive manner I could, they again dispersed.

I have not related these incidents, because they are not only descriptive of the factious spirit that prevailed, and how plausibly private pique could assume the appearance of public spirit, but tend likewise to show, that formidable as the republican party was, the loyalists were not less so; and that had it not been for the after impediment, of a long and rigorous imprisonment, I should undoubtedly have had the power, by collecting, encouraging, and heading my friends, to have served my king and country most essentially.

Once more at liberty, I had now to pursue my plan of visiting Lord Dunmore; but the distance I had to travel, and the lawless and suspicious temper of the times, made this no easy matter. The treaty which I had concluded with the Indians, gave me ostensible business to the Committee at Winchester; and the better to hide my intentions, I prevailed with three of the Indian Chiefs to accompany me thither, carrying with me a copy of the treaty, calculated for the inspection of the President and Convention assembled at Richmond. I travelled about one hundred and eighty miles from Fort Pitt, till I came to the warm springs in Frederick county, without any remarkable occurrence. Here I met a great concourse of Gentlemen from the different governments, who delivered sentiments very opposite to mine; but though I had the caution not to contradict, notwithstanding that I heard the grossest falsehoods industriously propagated, yet my silence was construed into dissension, and I was given to understand, I was a suspected person, and that it had been proposed to form a committee to enquire into my conduct and intentions. Though his arbitrary examination was dropped, I learnt, that several Gentlemen had written to the Committee at Winchester, describing me as a suspicious and dangerous character. I determined, however, to proceed; and concluded, that if I could escape, with plausibility, this one more difficulty,

I might obtain some certificate of the satisfaction my conduct had given this newly erected tribunal, which might serve as a passport through the remainder of my journey.

The day after I arrived, the expected scrutiny took place, and I found not only the letters written from the suspicious valetudinarians of the warm springs, but one come express from the clerk of the county where I myself presided, replete with assurances to the committee, of my dangerous and Tory principles; and expressive of a conviction, that I intended to join Lord Dunmore, and meditated every opposition to the laudable purposes then adopted for the suppression of tyranny. To men enflamed with enthusiastic ideas of infringed rights, this was a charge most criminal: I endeavoured to avert and soften it, by declaring, first, in general terms, that though my reverence for the King and Constitution might, at some moments, possibly have betrayed me into expressions reflecting on certain proceedings, which I could not help dreading, might plunge our unhappy country into all the horrors of a civil war, yet I had ever exerted myself to the utmost extent of my abilities for the public good, in all affairs which I had been deemed worthy to transact: that I flattered myself, the treaty and proceedings with the Indians, now open for their inspection, would vouch for my assertions: that with respect to letters and suspicions, they were no proofs; and that the letter most positive in accusation, came from a person not instigated by a love of justice and his country, but by motives far less praiseworthy, of which I gave them satisfactory and notorious proofs.

And now an incident happened, that turned the scale entirely in my favour, for just as the Clerk of the Committee had finished reading the Indian treaty, an express arrived with dispatches from the President of the Convention, held at Richmond, containing not only entire approbation of my conduct, in the beforementioned Indian treaty, of which the Commissioners, sent to inspect and assist, had given an account, but likewise a polite and complimentary letter from the President to me, expressing a desire to see me along

2

with the Indian Chiefs. This produced everything I could wish. The Clerk was ordered to give me a copy of a resolve, signifying their entire satisfaction, at my good and able conduct, and their belief, of my having acted heretofore, in a manner conducive to the liberties of America.

It was not my purpose, however, to visit the convention, but Lord Dunmore : the next day, therefore, I informed the Indians, I must now part with them, as my business required I should take a different route ; advised them to meet the Convention at Richmond ; brought to their recollection, the duty I had so often inculcated, and took my leave ; but not without regret at parting with men, who, though unpolished and barbarous, had great integrity of heart, and an inviolable friendship.

So full was the country become of Committees, new raised militia, petty officers, and other persons officially busy, in hopes of being distinguished, that the utmost circumspection was continually necessary. When I came to Fredericksburg, I dined with an old friend, in better days Doctor, afterwards General Mercer, and killed at Prince Town, in an action with the seventeenth regiment, and because I was silent, when inflammatory and unconstitutional toasts and sentiments were drank, the next day, when I again set off on my journey, I found they had placed a spy upon me, under the appearance of an accidental traveller on the road to Richmond.

Him, however, I had the address to shake off. When I came near Williamsburg, I contrived so as to pass through the town in the night. I saw several officers and soldiers, and was hailed by the centinels, but answering, "a friend," they supposed me a country Gentleman, and suffered me to pass. Though the rains had been, and were exceedingly heavy, attended with violent thunder and lightning, I did not stop till I came to York-Town, which was towards midnight, and there, thoroughly drenched, and excessively fatigued, I went to bed. Being near the end of my journey, on the morning I set forward, through still unremitting rain, which, though very disagreeable, was a very convenient circumstance, for the militia and inhabitants were obliged to keep in their houses, and I passed through Hampton safe and unobserved. I here procured a boat, and by a little finesse with the waterman, got on board the ship where Lord Dunmore usually remained. His Lordship was gone on shore to Gosport, whither I instantly followed, and immediately obtained the ardently wished-for-pleasure of an interview.

Those only who have seen such times, and been in similar situations; who have felt the like passionate desire to distinguish themselves in the service of their King and country, and the like apprehensions of being prevented, those only can conceive the satisfaction I experienced at this moment. I had been twice a prisoner, twice rescued; had passed the Apalachian Mountains, and come upwards of four hundred and fifty miles, through a country where every eye seemed intuitively suspicious; had formed a party in favour of the cause I had espoused; and my heart swelled with the hopes of doing something eminently conspicuous: I had happily joined a Nobleman, whose loyal sentiments corresponded with my own, and who made it an invariable rule never to suffer those who preferred their allegiance to the vain applause of a giddy multitude, to pass undistinguished. Thus far success attended my efforts, and I was happy: the reverse of the medal must presently appear.

It was evident, on consulting with Lord Dunmore, and informing him of the plan I had concerted, and the confederacy I had formed, that when his Lordship was reinforced with supplies from Britain, a co-operative body of troops from Canada, and the western frontiers of Virginia, with Indian auxiliaries, would be ready to act at the time that Sir William Howe would draw their principal attention to the northward. This would not only be productive of the restitution of the royal authority of this colony, but have a general tendency to promote the success of his Majesty's arms, and the like happy effects universally. His Lordship therefore dispatched me to General Gage at Boston, to lay before his Excellency the projected scheme, and to desire his concurrence and co-operation.   But as Lord Dunmore had promised the Indian Chiefs, when in their country, that he would certainly meet them in person the ensuing spring, at Fort Pitt, finally to adjust all differences; and as the rebellion had rendered it impossible to keep his promise, he was solicitous to transmit an apology to a Chief of the Delawares, intimating in some measure the cause of this disappointment.   This speech his Lordship gave to my charge, and desired me to transmit to a Mr. Gibson, of Pittsburgh, that he might interpret it to the Chief.   I had reason to suspect Lord Dunmore reposed too much confidence in this Gentleman, but as he had lately been with his Lordship on business, and as his Lordship seemed persuaded he was worthy of being trusted, I gave up suspicions that afterwards appeared to be but too well founded.   Ideas of former intimacy and juvenile friendship arose in my mind, for we had been long acquainted, and I felt an anxiety to preserve him from measures, which I deemed destructive to both his interest and honour.   When therefore I sent him the speech, I likewise enclosed the following letter:

PORTSMOUTH, Aug. 9, 1775.

DEAR SIR.

I am safely arrived here, and am happy, to the greatest degree, in having so fortunately escaped the narrow inspection of my enemies, the enemies to their country, to good order, and to government.   I should esteem myself defective in point of friendship towards you, should I neglect to caution you to avoid an over zealous exertion of what is now ridiculously called patriotic spirit : but, on the contrary, to deport yourself with that moderation for which you have always been remarkable, and which must, in this instance, tend to your honour and advantage.

You may be assured from me, Sir, that nothing but the greatest unanimity now prevails at home; that the innovating spirit amongst us here is looked upon as ungenerous and undutiful; that the utmost exertions of the powers

of government, if necessary, will be used to convince the
infatuated people of their folly. I could, I assure you, Sir,
give you such convincing proofs of what I assert, and from
which every reasonable person may conclude the effects,
that nothing but madness could operate upon a man so far
as to overlook his duty to the present constitution, and to
form unwarrantable associations with enthusiasts, whose ill-
timed folly must draw upon them inevitable destruction.
His Lordship desires you to present his hand to Capt.
White-Eyes, and to assure him that he is very sorry he had
not the pleasure of seeing him at the treaty, or that the situation of affairs prevented him from coming down. Believe
me, dear Sir, that I have no motive in writing my sentiments
thus to you, farther than to endeavour to steer you clear of
the misfortunes which I am confident must involve, but
unhappily, too many.

I have sent you an address from the People of Great-
Britain to the People of America; and I desire you to consider it attentively, which will, I flatter myself, convince you
of the idleness of many declamations, and of the absurdity
of an intended slavery. Give my love to George, and tell
him he shall hear from me, and I hope to his advantage.
Interpret the inclosed speech to Capt. White-Eyes from his
Lordship; be prevailed upon to shun the popular error, and
judge for yourself; act as a good subject, and expect the
rewards due to your services.

I am, dear Sir,
Your sincere friend and servant,
JOHN CONNOLLY.

To JOHN GIBSON, ESQUIRE,
near Fort Dunmore.

To a mind impressed with the slightest sense of rectitude,
and that has ever once conceived the meaning of the word
honour, it seems impossible that any man can be base enough
to betray a private confidential correspondence, more espe-
cially where the intention was indisputably benevolent and
friendly. This dishonourable act, however, was Mr. Gib-

son's: he laid my letter before the county committee, to which I am to attribute my succeeding misfortunes, and a five years' captivity. Many other letters of mine were sent, at the same time, and by the same conveyance, to persons who afterwards accepted offices of high trust under the Republican government; yet none, either then or since, ever divulged my opinions. This gentleman, for his treacherous display of patriotism, was honoured with a consequential military command; and I have frequently had the mortification to see him enjoy the warm sun-shine of freedom and favour, from the window of an inhospitable prison. But to return.

It was agreed that I should go to Boston, for which voyage a small schooner was provided and manned from the Otter Sloop, and I set out for head quarters, charged with Lord Dunmore's dispatches to the commander in chief, where I arrived after a voyage of ten days.

Secret and expeditious as I had hitherto been, my arrival at Boston was soon known to General Washington. The inhabitants, by permission, were daily going in and out of town; and some of them had so far corrupted my servant, as to obtain from him such intelligence as he could give. He was an Englishman, had lived with Lord Dunmore, and had acquaintance in General Washington's family, to whom, some short time after, he eloped, where he reported a strange mixture of truth and falsehood, relative to my past proceedings and future intentions.

When my propositions were laid before General Gage, [as] he was well acquainted with American affairs, and saw the advantages that were likely to result from their being put in execution: they met, therefore, with his entire approbation. But as General Arnold (then in the American service) had already began an expedition against Canada by the Kennebec River, and other obstacles intervened, I could not immediately proceed to Quebec, as was at first intended, so it was thought most expedient I should return to Virginia, taking with me his Excellency's instructions to the officers commanding at Illinois and Detroit, as well as to the deputy superintendent of Indian affairs.

After experiencing several of those tedious delays always inseparable from sea voyages, and calling on board the Asia, lying at New York, agreeable to the directions of Lord Dunmore, to enquire for dispatches from England, I arrived once more at Portsmouth, and rejoined his Lordship on the 12th of October. A short fit of sickness, occasioned by excessive fatigue and anxiety, for I had travelled this year upwards of four thousand miles, and always upon affairs that lay heavy on the mind, held me in a suspense that, while it lasted, made illness doubly irksome. As soon, however, as I was able, I consulted with his Lordship upon my plan and future proceedings; and on the 5th of November, 1775, a commission of Lieutenant-Colonel Commandant under his Lordship's sign manual, as his Majesty's representative, was given me, with full power and authority to raise a battalion of men, and as many independent companies as I could. The deputy superintendent of Indian affairs was directed to make such expences in that department, as I might judge requisite for his Majesty's service; and the officer commanding a detachment of the eighteenth regiment at the Illinois, was ordered to join me at Detroit, by the Onabache communication. The commanding officer at Detroit, likewise, was desired to give every encouragement to the Canadians of his district, to embody themselves for the expedition under my orders; and every other matter was so arranged, as to give the fairest prospect of success. These dispositions were made conformable to appearances and probabilities. Early the next spring, we had the strongest reason to hope, that a formidable body of British troops would take the field; that the combined force of the enemy must be drawn to the northward, and that I should have an opportunity of marching from Pittsburgh, with the detachment of the eighteenth regiment, the new-raised corps, the Indian auxiliaries, so as to form a junction with Lord Dunmore at Alexandria. By this means the communication between the southern and northern governments would have been interrupted, and a favourable turn indisputably given to his Majesty's affairs in the southern Provinces.

To put these designs into action, the service required I should first go to Detroit, to gain which there were several routes. But as this garrison lay at least seven hundred miles distant in the straightest possible direction, and as the circuitous roads were not only very tedious, but liable to other objections, I determined to go the shortest way through Maryland. In this my knowledge of the country and the people, made me so far justifiable, that I should undoubtedly have succeeded, and passed safe, had it not been for an accident (before alluded to) of which I could not then possibly have any foresight. My instructions and commission were concealed in the sticks of my servant's mail pillion, artfully contrived for that purpose, and in the night of the 13th of November, 1775, I took my leave of Lord Dunmore, and set off in company with Lieutenant Allen Cameron, and Dr. John Smyth. These Gentlemen were both staunch loyalists, men of abilities, and very agreeable to me. Mr. Cameron was from Scotland, and well acquainted with the Indians and Indian affairs, having acted as agent under the honourable John Stuart, superintendent general of the department. He had suffered much abuse for his unshaken loyalty, previous to his coming into Virginia, and had refused the republican offers of military rank in South Carolina with disdain. He had come with dispatches from Governor Lord William Campbell, of South Carolina, Tonyn of East Florida, and the honourable John Stuart, and intended to serve in a corps of Highland emigrants, then raising at Boston, and since the eighty-fourth regiment. His loyalty, courage and good conduct, were so well established, that Lord Dunmore thought him a proper person to accompany me, and gave him a lieutenant's commission, leaving it with me to advance him to a company, if I thought good, on raising the corps, which from the experience I afterwards had of his worth and estimable qualities, I should certainly have done. Dr. Smyth was a Gentleman, who had resided in Maryland, but his nonconformity to the temper of the times, had made him obnoxious to the republican party. Incapable of temporizing he was on his way to West Florida, to escape the turbulence of faction, and act agreeably to his principles. Observing him to be a man of quick penetration, firm loyalty, and ready to serve his Majesty at all hazards, intimately acquainted too with the lower parts of Maryland, through which I intended to pass, I solicited him to accompany me likewise, designing to make him surgeon to the regiment.

We began our unfortunate journey by the way of the Potomac River, intending to land on the Maryland side near Port Tobacco, and by a feint, leave the Pittsburgh road, and proceed by a private route to a place called the Standing Stone, which was beyond the influence of county committees, and from whence to Detroit is not above seven days journey. This, however, was prevented by a furious north-west wind, that drove us up the river St. Mary's, where we landed and took the road like ordinary travellers. We proceeded on, unmolested, till the evening of the 19th, when we were on the very border of the frontier, and almost out of danger. We stopped for the night at a public house about five miles beyond Hager's Town, the landlord of which knew me. From him we learnt, that although it was known I had been on board with Lord Dunmore, yet it was supposed I should return quietly to Pittsburgh, as soon as I had settled my own personal concerns; neither was it known that I had been to Boston. The misfortune that hung over my head was the effect, not of temerity, but unsuspected private treachery, and the manner in which this happened was as follows :

Some short time before we came to our inn in the evening, a young man met us, that had formerly been a private under my command at Pittsburgh, and saluted me as he passed, by the title of major. This gave some uneasiness to the gentlemen with me, who wished to have him secured ; but as I could not pass through the country without the probability of being known by many, and as any violence, or even art, used with the man, were likely rather to produce than avoid the effects they feared ; beside, that there was not really any probable danger, I thought it by far more prudent to suffer him to pass unnoticed. About ten o'clock

the same night, this man went to a beer-house in Hager's
Town, and mixed with some officers of the Minute-men (a
species of the Volunteer Militia) where hearing some person in company enquire who those gentlemen were that
passed through the town in the evening, he replied, that one
of them was Major Connolly.   Unfortunately for me a copy
of my letter to Mr. Gibson, with Lord Dunmore's speech to
the Delaware Chief, had been sent, only two days before, to
the Colonel of the Minute-Men, who had spoken of it as a
demonstration of my Tory principles to the officers then
present; they, therefore, immediately informed their Colonel
of my having passed through the town, and he, with as much
expedition, sent a body of his men after us, to oblige us to
return, that we might be examined before the committee.
About two o'clock in the morning they suddenly broke into
the room where we lay, and made us prisoners.   We were
conducted to Hager's Town, kept in separate houses during
the next day and night, and suffered that kind of disturbance
and abuse which might be expected from undisciplined soldiers, and a clamorous rabble, at such a crisis.   The day
following, the committee being assembled, my letter was
produced, as a testimony of my political principles being
repugnant to their own; and the speech of Lord Dunmore
commented upon, as designed to influence the Indians to
act against them, in case of hostilities with Great Britain.
To which I answered, the sentiments contained in my letter
were the result of friendship for a person, with whom I had
had a long and early acquaintance.   They were not calculated to publicly prejudice their measures; and the person
advised was entirely at liberty to pursue his own inclinations.
It extended no farther than the giving a private opinion;
and the only person culpable was he who could so unwar-
rantably betray a confidential letter.   With respect to the
speech, I observed, it was merely an apology from Lord
Dunmore to the Indians; he not being able to meet them in
council at Pittsburgh, agreeable to his promise the preceding
year.   The heat of party resentment seemed considerably
abated when they had heard me; but it was nevertheless

resolved, I should not proceed home (where they supposed me going) till the sense of the whole committee, assembled at Frederick Town, could be taken. This fatal resolution, carried only by a small majority, was, I foresaw, destruction to my hopes, as the news of my having been at Boston must soon get abroad.

And now, instead of proceeding in the service to which my heart was devoted, the next day we were escorted back to Frederick Town, about thirty-five miles, in a retrograde direction, from where we were taken. Here, the first house I entered, I saw a Colonel well known to me, who had just returned from before Boston, and who proceeded, without hesitation, to inform me, that General Washington knew the time of my coming to, and the very day of my leaving Boston; and that it was generally supposed I intended getting into the western part of the Quebec government by the Mississippi. All attempts at denial were now idle.

The committee were anxious to seize my papers; but, as I found their search ineffectual, I told them they had been sent to Quebec; and, after repeated examination, my portmanteau was returned to my servant, without discovery. Yet, although Dr. Smyth and myself had several times, before we left Norfolk, severely scrutinized and destroyed every paper that might affect us, there was a manuscript that had been wrapt round a stick of black ball by my servant, so soiled and besmeared, as to have escaped the search both of ourselves there, and the committee here, who were as industrious as they were suspicious. This paper, which contained a rough draft of propositions, supposed to have been laid before General Gage by me, but which really was not the case, was discovered in consequence of a fresh examination demanded by a Member of Congress, who arrived at the committee some days after we had been taken to Frederick Town, and was published as my confession, though I repeatedly, and with truth, denied the justice of the supposition.

We were now decidedly prisoners, and it became one of

my chief concerns lest my friends of West Augusta County might suffer from my misfortune. I, therefore, obtained an interview with the Member of Congress, and endeavoured to eradicate every suspicion from his mind, by introducing such conversation as I judged most conducive to this purpose. Among other matters, this gentleman informed me, that Congress seeing the consequences of civil war inevitable, had come to a determination that officers taken by them should be admitted to their parole, and treated with every lenity consistent with the public interest, as they expected a similar indulgence would be extended to the unfortunate on their side, who should become prisoners. How far this resolution was adhered to, the subsequent part of this narrative will testify. The idea was, indeed, to me very renovating; it gave me to hope, that although a prisoner now, and my efforts for the present impeded, I should soon regain my liberty, and have still the power to prove myself an active supporter of the constitutional government.

We were now removed to the house of the Colonel of the Minute-men, and confined in a room where we had no reason to complain of lodging, or diet; but the clamorous gabbling of this raw militia was eternal and noisy beyond conception. They were ignorant, and stupidly turbulent; and their guard, which was relieved every four-and-twenty hours, gave a night of entertainment to themselves and visitors, and of tantalizing perturbation to me, whose heart was incessantly panting after other scenes, and different companions.

My servant, who was a man of great fidelity and adroitness, was not confined; and as he had gathered some slight intimation that matters of consequence were in the pillion sticks, and observing the saddle and its appendages suspended in an adjoining shed, after having undergone a severe but fruitless scrutiny by the committee, he seized a favourable moment in the dead of night, opened the sticks, examined their contents by the light of a fire, and finding of what importance they were, destroyed them all, except my commission. This he sealed up, and conveyed to me, with a note informing me of what he had done, by means of a negro girl, that had before been proved to bo faithful.

Among other conjectures, on the probable operations of Congress, I began to reflect, that they would certainly send a body of men down the Ohio, to capture the small garrison at Kuskuskis, as they were in great want of stores and ordnance. I therefore wished very much to inform Captain Lord, who commanded at the Illinois, of his imminent danger, and advise him to quit his post, and gain Detroit, by the Onabache communication, without delay. We had observed, that towards day-light, our guard frequently exhausted by their own noise and folly, were inclined to a momentary quiet, and as no centry were regularly relieved, but all were on duty at the same time, we concluded there was a possibility for one of my companions to effect an escape. But as verbal intelligence might not find immediate credit, it was necessary I should write, and in this our good negro again assisted us: she procured paper, and an ink-horn, which she contrived to leave between the bed and sacking-bottom, unnoticed by the guard. Thus furnished, I wrote the necessary letters, and Dr. Smyth willingly offering his services for this laborious undertaking, we contrived to unscrew the lock from the door, and towards morning, just as the guard were nodding in their chairs, he slipt down stairs unobserved. We had scarce time to screw the lock on again, and lie down, before the guard entered our room, but seeing some of us in bed, they concluded we were all there, so cried all safe, and retired. This business was very critically effected, for the next day we were to be removed towards Philadelphia, pursuant to an order of Congress.

In the morning, when it was found that Dr. Smyth had made his escape, we felt such consequences as might naturally be expected from vulgar and exasperated men, and were plentifully loaded with opprobrious epithets.

It was on the 29th of December, 1775, in a severely cold season of the year, that we set out for Philadelphia, a journey of one hundred and sixty miles. We were escorted by a party of militia dragoons; our spurs were taken off, our

horses placed parallel like coach horses, with their heads
tied together in a very confined manner, and a horseman,
with a long rope attached to the intermediate cord, rode
before, rudely conducting us in whatever direction he
thought proper. My servant was allowed to follow with
my portmanteau, but not having taken off his spurs, the
populace ran violently up to him, and cut through his boot
and stocking to tear them away. We were obliged to perform a considerable journey that day, in a manner painful
to remember; the road was rough, the snow on the ground,
the rivulets numerous and frozen, and a track for the horses
obliged to be broken through them. These were only made
wide enough for a single horse, and notwithstanding our
entreaties to the contrary, we were obliged to enter all these
narrow passes, with our horses abreast, the consequence of
which was, a continual contest between the poor animals, to
preserve the open communication, alternately forcing each
other to jump upon the firm ice, or break a larger extent in
the struggle. Our knees were repeatedly bruised, and our
limbs in imminent danger of being broken, by the incessant falls and warfare of the horses. Sorry am I to say,
it rather afforded cause of merriment to our conductors,
than any scope for the exercise of benevolence. For the
honour of humanity, however, it should be observed, that
our guard consisted of the lowest and most irrational of the
inhabitants, in and near the town of Frederick, and their
captain a common surgeon-barber.

On the second day we reached York Town, where a committee assembled to determine how they were to lodge us.
Their deliberations were not of long continuance; we were
committed to a room in the county gaol, in which was a
dirty straw bed, little covering; and, notwithstanding the
inclemency of the season, no fire; add to which, their new
made soldiers were so fond of fife and drum, that they entertained us all night with this music. The next morning
was the first of January, 1776, and we were conducted from
gaol to the tavern, where our horses were, by an officer's
guard, and a drum beating the rogue's march. Here we

were consigned once more to our polite friends of Frederick Town, who, to the no small entertainment of the populace, ironically and vociferously complimented us with many wishes of a happy new year.

Led in this insulting manner, by a formidable guard, and exhibited *in terrorem* to all loyalists, I now too plainly saw the probability of my falling a political sacrifice, and that this parade of indignity was but the commencement of my sufferings. I was the first person of influence, who had attempted to support the Royal cause, by raising troops in America. That they meant to intimidate every Gentleman from future efforts of that nature, not only by exposing me as an object of contempt to one party, and of dread to the other, but of unrelenting persecution likewise, will I think be evident from the facts contained in this narrative. Let it, however, be always understood, both here, and in all other places, where I mention the rigours I sustained, that I do not mean to accuse any man, or set of men, any farther than a fair statement of my own case requires; nor have I any view, but to shew that my sufferings were the effects of my unshaken loyalty, that I was, while free, an active maintainer, and when imprisoned, an inflexible adherent to the cause I espoused; that they were convinced of this, and that this was the source of the unabating severity with which I was treated. By the received modes of modern war, their conduct was certainly unjustifiable; how far their peculiar situation may extenuate this charge, is not for me to determine. My purpose is only faithfully to relate what the interest of myself and family demands should be related.

When we again set forward, great numbers of the inhabitants of York-Town rode with us to Wright's-Ferry, as well for the novelty of the sight, as to be present at an interview that was expected to take place between me and an uterine brother of mine, who had long been the representative of the county in the general assembly of the Province, and who was of a very different political complexion. I know not how this meeting affected the multitude, but to me it conjured up a train of melancholy ideas; my own ex-

ample gave me a strong picture of the horrors of civil dis-
cord, that was too dismal to behold without a shudder. My
stay was short; at my brother's request, I was suffered to
walk upon the ice, across the Susquehanna, in his company,
with the guard following in the rear. The painful remembrance of the blessings of peace, and of the ravages of that
dissention that could make the brother war against the
brother, and the son against the father, gave sensations,
better to be imagined than expressed. When we reached
the opposite shore, therefore, we soon took our leave.

This night we were lodged in the gaol at Lancaster, and
two days more brought us to Philadelphia, where we were
committed to the charge of the associated city militia dressed
in uniform. About six in the evening, by an order from the
Council of Safety, we were marched to where they sat, and
from thence to prison, where, by the nature of the commit-
ment, we were debarred the use of pen, ink, and paper.
My servant too was now involved in the severity practised
upon me, and we were all three shut up in a dirty room, in
which we could obtain nothing but an old pair of blankets,
and that only in consideration of a considerable premium to
the gaoler. In this state we continued in the depth of
winter for ten days, without a change of linen, before we
could get our cloaths out of the hands of the Council of
Safety; at length they were restored, and by virtue of
pecuniary influence, we obtained something that the keeper
called a bed. Here we remained till the latter end of January, when we were removed to a new and elegant prison,
then lately erected, whither we were escorted with great
formality, and again honoured with a rogue's march. Was
this necessity, or was it illiberal faction? if the latter, success
will not surely wipe off the aspersion incurred by the author
of this ungenerous treatment; if the former, benevolence
must lament for those who were the unfortunate victims.
Thus Congress were determined, not only to hold me up
as a public example of political vengeance to the loyalists,
but to take every means possible to degrade and render me
contemptible.

Though I had progressively acquired rank in the provincial service, of which they could not be ignorant, few men having been more generally or more respectably acquainted in the middle and southern colonies, though I had obtained a lieutenant-colonel's commission under his Majesty, yet whenever they had occasion to mention me in their resolves and public proceedings, they wrote plain John Connolly, without the least mark of distinction, or affected to call me Doctor, thereby bringing to the remembrance of those who knew me, that it was once intended I should pursue the practice of physic, if that were any disgrace, and insinuating to the world at large, that a Doctor would not have been in such a situation, had he not been a busy, factious person. The English history is replete with instances of a similar nature. The tyranny and insolence of republican faction, arraigned even the sovereign of these realms, by the name of Charles Stuart. Self-defence obliges me to make the foregoing remarks, it would else become matter of wonder, when the papers of Congress necessarily cited hereafter come to be read, Why, if I were what I say, I was not so distinguished.

Amidst the hardships and chagrines I daily suffered, I had still the consolation to reflect, I had done every thing possible in the discharge of my duty, and anxiously hoped Mr. Smyth had been fortunate enough to escape to the Illinois, but in this I was disappointed. This Gentleman, after having encountered a variety of difficulties, and suffered abuses for having undertaken this enterprise, scandalous to the perpetrators, disagreeable to remember, and unnecessary to relate, was brought once more a prisoner to Philadelphia. I was still resolved, if possible, to apprize Captain Lord of his danger, which I effected by the following means.

The Council of Safety had made a resolution to discharge all British prisoners, privates, who would take an oath not to engage in hostilities against the United Colonies. Among their captives, was a recruit of the Highland emigrants, that was allowed to come of a morning to make my fire, whom

I found to be acute, and willing to do me any service. This man I prevailed on to take the oath, and procure his release, and then resolved to send him to Pittsburgh, with letters to a friend of mine, who might dispatch an Indian down the Ohio to Captain Lord. The recruit found opportunity to bring me some writing paper and sal ammoniac, and the business was happily effected. By this means I endeavoured to preserve his Majesty's garrison, stores, and ordnance; but as the transaction became ultimately known to Congress, it did not tend to lessen their severities.

When Mr. Cameron and myself were conveyed to the new Prison, we were both confined in one room; the walls were thick, and not thoroughly dry, so that we contracted inveterate colds. Our room door was constantly kept shut, and our windows towards the street nailed down, by which all free circulation of air was prevented, neither was any person suffered to speak to me, without an order under the signature of the Secretary of Congress. Under these circumstances, I began first to experience a very disagreeable and a very serious alteration in my health, when by a resolve of Congress, I was allowed more open air, and a separate room; but this indulgence was of short duration, and I was again locked up night and day.

In the month of December, 1776, an attempt was made by Mr. Cameron, Mr. Smyth, and another gentleman (Mr. Maclean, since captain in the Eighty-fourth), of so industrious and hazardous a nature as to deserve a particular relation, the horrors of their imprisonment alone can account for the temerity of the enterprize. These gentlemen, with wonderful exertions and address, and with no other tool but a knife, opened a hole through the arched roof, and got unobserved upon the top of the prison. With the unsound paillasses on which they lay, and their old blankets torn up, they made a rope, and perilous as the attempt too visibly was, resolved to endeavour this way to descend. Mr. Cameron, than whom no man is more daringly intrepid, made the first and the only essay; for scarce had he suspended himself beneath the roof, before the faithless cord broke, and he fell near fifty feet upon a hard frozen ground. It seems miraculous, that immediate death was not the consequence. He was taken up lifeless, his ancle bones were broken, and his whole frame shattered. The two unhurt gentlemen were thrown into the dungeon, where they remained until removed, with the other prisoners, to Baltimore, on the advance of the royal army to Trent Town, when Mr. Cameron, in a dying condition, was taken to the sick quarters in the city. Mr. Smyth was more fortunate in a third attempt, escaping from Baltimore to New York, where Sir William Howe gave him a company in the Queen's Rangers.

Mr. Cameron did not obtain his release till the winter of 1778, when, from a series of extreme hardships and abuses, his health was so much impaired, and he only enabled to walk on crutches, that he was incapable of service. This he accounted his greatest misfortune; he therefore came to England, bearing with him the most unequivocal and melancholy testimonials of his loyalty. Here he recovered in so astonishing a manner, that scarcely any visible marks of lameness remain. I am sorry to add, he has not been provided for in that mode in which he is again become capable of acting, with honour to himself, and advantage to society.

When Congress first fled from Philadelphia to Baltimore, they left only a small committee of their body to act in concert with the Council of Safety. I had now been immured within the inhospitable walls of a gaol for upwards of a year, deprived of all exercise, cut off from all social intercourse, and my mind preyed upon by eternal chagrine, by reiterated reflections on what I hoped to have performed, and what, were I free, I might still perform: no wonder that my state of health became truly deplorable. I had contracted a complication of disorders; my legs were swollen, and I was emaciated to a surprising degree. Solitude itself was become more solitary, for the very prison was deserted, and I only remained. At this crisis, two members of the Council of Safety came to inform me, I must prepare to move to the southward; to which I replied, that my health was so far impaired, of which they seeing me, would not avoid being convinced, I was no longer able to encounter the difficulties to which I saw others exposed, and that if they meant to continue my existence, they must suffer me to procure a carriage, and go on my parole. To this they assented, moved, as I imagined, by the spectacle they beheld; and I was in hourly expectation of a partial relief, which, however, I did not obtain, till my brother, now become a General in the service of Congress, came to command at Philadelphia. Through his interest, and becoming responsible for my appearance when demanded, I was enlarged upon my parole, and sent to his house in the country, where I was allowed five miles distance to ride for the recovery of my health. This was fourteen months after my first becoming a prisoner at Hager's town.

I remained here between five and six weeks, and was then remanded back to prison, where I continued about six weeks longer, with the liberty, however, of walking in the gaol yard during the day. My health had been too radically impaired to be so suddenly re-established, which being represented to Congress, I was again admitted to live at my brother's on my parole, though not till he had entered into a high pecuniary obligation with the Council of Safety for my appearance.

I now began to hope, that austerity and persecution were past, and that henceforth I should be allowed something like those liberties which officers, under such circumstances, usually enjoy, till my exchange could be effected. I was miserably deceived. I continued, in this comparatively happy situation from the 11th of April, 1777, till the 14th of October following, when Congress, once more obliged to fly from Philadelphia at the approach of Sir William Howe, retired to York Town, in the vicinity of my brother's house. The night of the 14th I was again apprehended, by an order from the board of war: my papers, with every scrap of manuscript they could collect, seized, and myself hurried away to York-Town prison, close locked up, and every former severity renewed. I was conscious of having done

nothing to merit this treatment, and imagined, that as it
might flow from some malicious misrepresentation of my
having given secret intelligence to the British army, I should
be enlarged as soon as my innocence appeared. But my
prediction was drawn from reflections on justice, candour,
and humanity, and I was a false prophet. My papers were
returned, and I was taught to hope for my former indulgence; but days and months elapsed, and I was still a
prisoner. The convention of Saratoga put so many persons of consequence into the possession of Congress, that
the prospect of either humane usage, or exchange, was very
faint.

In consequence of a recommendation from Congress, laws
were passed in some Provinces, that whoever among the
Loyalists should return, within a time specified, and become
subject to the Republic, should have their estates restored.
When this act took place in Virginia, I was earnestly solicited to renounce my allegiance, and again enjoy my lands
and liberty. But harrassed as I had been, and unhappy
as I was, without one earthly comfort, and scarce a future
ray of hope, this proposition was peremptorily rejected:
at the risk of a lingering death, I preferred my honour
and my loyalty to every inferior consideration. I was debarred the rights, but could not forget the duties of a good
subject.

York-Town gaol, where I was now confined, was so
crowded with British prisoners, it being the stage for such
as were marching southward, exclusive of those that were
resident, that at length a contagious fever appeared. About
this time Congress appointed a day of thanksgiving to be
observed throughout the United States, and their proclama-
tion was replete with professions of piety, benevolence, and
charity towards their enemies. This I thought a proper
time, by a firm and candid representation of facts, to draw
their attention towards the miserable condition of the
prison, and, in concurrence with the opinion of some
officers who signed the paper, I wrote and sent them the
following remonstrance:

To the Hon. Henry Laurens, Esq.:

May it please your Honour, We the subscribing persons, prisoners of war, having underwent a series of calamitous confinement equal to the utmost rigour (which has given cause to loud complaint) had the pleasing prospect of seeing a period to such afflictions by an exchange of officers, or by that humane interposition, which, in such cases, marks the character of a civilized and Christian people; but unhappily find ourselves disappointed. We beg leave to remind your Honour, of the multitude of prisoners taken by his Majesty's forces, who have been restored to their friends, and their distress alleviated by a dismission from captivity. Whilst we have beheld a succession of such events extending to almost all ranks of American prisoners, we are sorry to say, that our miseries have been aggravated by a most criminal imprisonment, in a loathsome, crowded jail infected with a contagious fever, and polluted with noisome smells through every part. Could any motives, founded upon reasons even of a political nature, be urged in justification of the treatment we experience, it would appear to us less objectionable; but when we are satisfied that different gentlemen, in every respect in similar circumstances with ourselves, who were born and educated in this country, have been admitted to generous favours, sent into the British lines, either on parole, or exchanged, and, in every other respect, treated only as unfortunate, we find ourselves utterly at a loss to account for the peculiarity of our persecution. In your address to the inhabitants of the United States, it is therein publicly declared, that you have studiously endeavoured to alleviate the captivity of your enemies. We most heartily wish we could subscribe to this assertion; but how is it possible, when sixteen months imprisonment, of the most distressing nature, is the shortest time of which any of us complain? Subject to all the indignities, and low insults, of an illiberal gaoler and turnkey, and placed upon the same footing with horse-thieves, deserters, negroes, and the lowest and most despicable of the human race? To cultivate the assistance of Heaven by acts which Heaven opposes, is a recommendation truly laudable. But whether the complaints which we thus exhibit, can be agreeable to the benignity of the Divine Ruler of Heaven, we submit to the dispassionate determination of your Honour. We beg leave, finally, to observe, that as this gaol is a stage for all prisoners moving to the westward, that such as are sick, lame, or otherwise disabled, are left behind, and as the yard, and every part of it, is truly odious, from the disagreeable smell, and unfit to maintain life, we intreat your Honour to lay this our Remonstrance before Congress, earnestly soliciting them to admit us to our paroles in any part of the country, or in some other manner to extend their humanity towards us, which, from our sufferings and your declarations, we have the greatest reasons to expect.

We are, Sir,

Your most obedient,

Humble servants,

JOHN CONNOLLY,
RICHARD W^M STOCKTON,
CHARLES HARRISON,
ASHER DUNHAM,
ROBERT MORRIS,
FRANCIS FRAGER.

YORK-TOWN GAOL, May 17, 1778.

This Address was productive of the following Resolve of Congress, and Report from the Board of War:

IN CONGRESS, May 23d, 1778.

Whereas it appears probable that attempts are making to misrepresent the conduct of these United States towards the prisoners in their possession, in some degree, to wipe off or counterbalance the just reproach that has fallen upon our enemies for their barbarity.

Resolved, That the letter from John Connolly and others, dated York-Town gaol, May the 17th, 1778, together with the report of the Board of War upon it, be published.

At a Board of War, 22d of May, 1778. The Board,

having taken into consideration the letter from Doctor John
Connolly, and the other prisoners of war, most of whom
have been lately removed from Carlisle gaol, into the prison
of the County of York, beg leave to report to Congress :

That, forbearing to remark upon the indecency of the
terms in which the said letter is conceived, and which is
calculated for other purposes than merely to relate their
pretended grievances, the board will lay before Congress the
facts which they have collected from Major Wilson, commanding at Carlisle, during the residence of Major Stockton, and other officers of his party in the gaol of that place.
. . . From Mr. Thomas Peters, Deputy Commissary of
prisoners, who had the charge during the winter, of the
prisoners at Carlisle and York, from Doctor Henry, employed to attend the British prisoners, when sick . . . and
from Colonel Pickering, one of the board, who visited
the gaol of this place. From the concurrent testimony
of all which gentlemen, the account given by the prisoners,
in the said letter, appears to be founded in misrepresentation.

Major Wilson, who was frequently called in by the officers
themselves to examine their situation at Carlisle, agrees with
the Commissary of prisoners.

That as often as either of these gentlemen visited the
gaol at Carlisle, the officers, being six in number, had the
privilege of the whole gaol, except such part as the gaoler
occupied, and one room entirely to themselves; and,
although the criminals were under the same roof, yet they
were so far from being crowded, that there were not in the
said gaol more than six or seven prisoners at a time (and
the most of these Tories) on an average, during the confinement of the officers at that place. That the gaol was as
clean as such places can be kept; and if it had not been so,
the fault would have lain with the officers, who were indulged with two servants to attend them for the purposes
of cleansing their apartment, and waiting on their persons.
These officers too, were confined by order of the Commissary General of prisoners, as a retaliation for those of our

army suffering every degree of insult and cruelty, which British haughtiness and inhumanity could inflict, in the provost and dungeons of New York and Philadelphia. This being the reason of their confinement, and the foregoing the situation of it, the board conceive their imprisonment was of the mildest nature, when compared with the rigours of that of our own officers. . . . But the gaol at Carlisle not being secure, the Deputy Commissary of prisoners, removed them to the prison of this place, wherein was confined Doctor John Connolly, for the same causes which induced and continue their present imprisonment; and for other reasons of policy and prudence, Doctor Connolly having also sundry times behaved amiss while on parole.

In the gaol at York, these prisoners (seven only in number) have two airy rooms; the one fifteen by twenty feet, and the other something less, besides the privilege of the whole gaol yard, which is sixty yards long, and eighteen wide . . . frequently swept, and kept as clean as possible, and by no means polluted with filth, &c., there being a privy at the extreme end of the yard. These gentlemen too, have three servants to attend them . . . their complaints, then, of being confined in a loathsome, crowded prison, infected with a contagious fever, and polluted with noisome smells through every part, are not warranted by facts. The gaol is made a place of temporary confinement for passing prisoners, but is never crowded, and there are now only nine privates therein, and three of them are the officers' servants, although it is capable of holding, conveniently, one hundred and sixty prisoners. There was, some time ago, an apprehension, in a part of the gaol, distant from the officers' apartments, that a contagious fever had broke out among the soldiers: but the diseased were immediately removed to hospitals, and a surgeon and nurses provided for them, and every assistance offered them the nature of our affairs would admit. The gaol is now clean and healthy, save that there are five soldiers who have fevers, from want of exercise and other causes common to

4

places of confinement; but the disorders are not contagious or dangerous.

Mr. Connolly, although indulged with every thing a prisoner could reasonably wish, has repeatedly represented his own, and the situation of the gaol, in similar terms with the letter now under consideration; and the former, and this board, have often had consequent examinations, in all of which, they found the complaints groundless. . . . Once, particularly, when Mr. Connolly represented himself at the point of death from the severity of his confinement, the board directed Doctor Shippen to visit him, who reported that his situation was directly opposite to his representation; his indisposition slight, and merely of an hypochondriac nature; the board have been so particular for several reasons, one whereof is, to supercede the necessity of future enquiries; and are upon the whole of opinion, that these gentlemen should be more strictly confined, as from the indulgence now given them, there is a probability of some of them, at least, making their escape.

By order of the Board,

RICHARD PETER.

Published by order of Congress,

CHARLES THOMPSON, *Secretary.*

Nothing can have a greater appearance of dispassionate candour, if we except the expression Tories, than this report: yet nothing was ever more abundant in chicane and deceit. On the 17th of May, the date of our letter, the gaol was exactly, literally, in the state we represented it to be: on the 23d of the same month it was what their report affirms. But, in the interim, so industrious were they to give their proceedings every appearance of truth, as well as of humanity, one hundred and fifty privates had been sent away, some of the sick removed, the gaol-yard thoroughly cleaned, and our rooms whitewashed. They then, with an ostentatious formality, examined the prison, and made their report. But was it probable, was it possible, that men could have the temerity, knowing themselves in the power of an unforgiving enemy, or the audacity, making pretension to the character of gentlemen, to affirm such direct falsehoods as their report made our letter to contain? Or if one were so spleen-ridden, as to magnify his miseries so excessively, would five other gentlemen have written their names, and disgraced themselves in attestation of his visions? No: Rouzed by a retrospection of things that could not be justified, and irritated that men should dare to speak the plain truth, they remove, in some measure, the cause of the complaint, and then affirm it never existed: they are afraid the tale should be told to their confusion, therefore resolve to tell it first themselves. No other excuse can be adduced to plead for the duplicity of their conduct, but the often reiterated one of political necessity. This, perhaps, may justify them to themselves, and to the world, as politicians, but will not invalidate my claim to distinction from the nation in whose cause I suffered. It will, likewise, if admitted, be a melancholy proof, that politics and justice are things, in their own nature, very distinct and heterogeneous.

There are other things in this report which I would wish should be particularly noticed. Retaliation, and *other* reasons of *policy* and *prudence*, are there assigned as the causes of my continued imprisonment. I hope this will be remembered, because very different motives are given hereafter. It is likewise there asserted, I had sundry times behaved amiss while on parole: this, upon the word and honour of a gentleman, I totally deny. I must, likewise, remark, that their other reasons of policy and prudence were evidently the conviction they had of my determination to leave nothing unessayed to serve his Majesty. They knew me to be an enterprizing, and, as may be adduced from the former part of this narrative, a dangerous enemy; and, therefore, would not suffer me to escape. These were reasons of policy and prudence.

Another effort is made to impugn my veracity, by saying, that Dr. Shippen, when he visited me, found my situation directly opposite to my representation: that my indisposition was slight, and merely of a hypochondriac nature. To this I answer, that when this visitation was made, I had lost my appetite; had an incessant watchfulness; was reduced to a skeleton; had blisters upon my neck; was incapable of walking across the room; and, for the two preceding nights, my brother officers had very humanely sat up with me. That melancholy and hypochondria should be generated in such a situation is not to be wondered at; but surely these were indications of something more than a slight indisposition.

Here, that is, in York-Town gaol, I remained till the evacuation of Philadelphia by the British army; when, just before the return of Congress to that city, I was informed, officially, that a general exchange had taken place, and that I, amongst others, was exchanged: but before the final departure of Congress, this information, though from the Board of War, was contradicted. Towards the latter end of July, a still stronger assurance of approaching liberty arrived. A letter from the American Commissary General of Prisoners came to York-Town, wherein it was required that I, with my brother officers, should be immediately forwarded to Elizabeth Town, to be exchanged. I was now admitted to my parole (be pleased to observe) *as a prisoner of war*, and obtained a passport for myself and servant to Philadelphia, when I waited on the Deputy Commissary of Prisoners, and shewed him my passport. He informed me, I should proceed in a day or two, took my address, and recommended me to keep within my lodgings. I was punctual in waiting upon him at the time mentioned, when to my utter surprize and chagrine, he told me, I was by order of Congress, to be again confined, for a few days, in the new gaol, until that body had more properly considered of the admission of my exchange, whither he had an officer in waiting to convey me. To have gained my parole, to be thus far advanced on my way, and afterwards, without the least cause, to be so cruelly and vexatiously again imprisoned, disturbed me so much, that I wrote to the President of Congress, complaining bitterly of the length of my confinement, and evidently studied cruelty of my treatment, to which I received no answer. I then addressed myself to General Washington, and stated the peculiarity of my case, who wrote me a short reply to this purport; "That he had transmitted my letter to the President of Congress, but could extend no relief to me, as I was the immediate prisoner of that body."

It was on the 5th of August, 1778, that I, for the third time, became an inhabitant of this prison, at which time I became acquainted with Captain Hawker, a Gentleman of great philanthropy and liberality of sentiment, and to whom I owe every acknowledgment, for his polite attentions and civilities while he remained.

My irritation of mind was now so great, that a dismal train of nervous disorders, established in my habit by former sufferings, were revived with such force, that sleep and appetite again forsook me, and I fell into the last stage of despondency. I wrote, however, on the 12th of October, to Congress, informed them of my ungenerous usage, and claimed the treatment of a prisoner of war. I ultimately demanded a personal audience of a Committee of Congress, in order to know wherefore I was refused to be exchanged, or on what pretence I had been subjected to such unparalleled injustice and indignities. The officers who signed the before recited remonstrance, were Provincial, not British officers, born and bred in America; and they, as well as many more in the same predicament, had been exchanged, therefore my country could be no impediment. Mr. Cameron, who had been taken with me at Hagar's Town, had been so also of course. I was upon that ground equally eligible. I therefore declared I was utterly incapable of accounting, by any mode of reasoning, for my peculiar detention, and required to receive personal and authentic information.

For once I was gratified, and brought before a committee, where having briefly recapitulated my causes of complaint, the chairman replied to the following purport:

That it had been for some time past his opinion, which he had not scrupled to communicate to Congress, that I should be kept in close custody, until Sir John Johnson was delivered up to them, who, he asserted, had broken his sacred parole given to General Scuyler, and joined the enemy; since which time he had been committing ravages upon the northern frontiers, with a body of light troops and Indians, as he supposed I intended to do.

To this I answered, that a parole or honorary obligation, I presumed, was of modern date, calculated to alleviate the horrors of war; that no Gentleman could be answerable for any but himself; that I had been admitted to my parole above a year ago, when my conduct was irreproachable, and that I was again, without the least cause on my part, thrown into prison, and there continued for another year; that much had been said about the infraction of my parole, which I utterly denied to have been the case.

To this they replied, I certainly had not adhered to the spirit of it, for that I had spoken against their proceedings, and had frequently attempted to turn them into ridicule.

I answered, the spirit of my parole was so indefinite a phrase, that it carried no accusation; that it was impossible to produce an instance, and that nothing of this nature could be affirmed, except in vague and general terms.

The final objection they made to my exchange, turned upon the impropriety of my being considered as a prisoner of war. They said, I had not been taken at the head of any armed troops, but privately making my way through the country; and one of them asserted, I might be considered as amenable to law martial, as a spy; but at the same time he observed, there was no intention of treating me as such.

This was an accusation of so strange and novel a nature, that it excited both my surprise and indignation; and I answered it, recapitulating, that I had been now almost three years a prisoner, in which space I had been three times admitted to my parole on their own authority; that I had repeatedly complained to them of the harshness of my treatment, and the length of my imprisonment, but

that they never before had alledged this crime against me
in their justification; nor was it, I said, possible, with even
a shadow of truth. I was the King's commissioned officer,
taken in the execution of my duty, to a sovereign, at that
time, acknowledged by themselves. America was not a
separate state; no independency was declared; no penal
laws promulgated. Neither was there anything to spy. I
was perfectly acquainted with the country, and there were
no armed troops, fortifications, or intrenchments, to be
inspected; nay, more, themselves knew my business was
not to give intelligence, but to act, which had been publicly
declared in their proceedings concerning me, in which I had
been acknowledged a prisoner of war.

The committee at length promised to consider and report
my case to Congress, and as my health was so exceedingly
and visibly impaired, gave me an intimation, that if I were
not exchanged, I should be enlarged on parole. I was then
re-conducted to prison.

As the sole end and purport of this narrative is to show,
that I was, from the commencement to the last moment,
firm and active in my loyalty; that had I been at liberty, I
had *the power* as well as *the will* to serve my sovereign and my
country; that Congress were conscious of this, and therefore resolved to detain me, which they did in an extraordinary manner, and quite distinct from any other Loyalist,
during the whole contest; I therefore hope my prolixities
will be forgiven, and my endeavours to exhibit myself and
sufferings such as they really were, considered not as the
effusions of vanity, but a strict and literal representation of
facts, in order to obtain justice: that I shall be indulged
with a patient hearing, while I contrast the assertions, and
shew the incongruities of the opposite party; and that,
while I "extenuate nought, nor aught set down in malice,"
I shall not be thought guilty of magnifying my own misfortunes, or the political injuries of my enemies.

Permit me then to remark, that in the report of the 23d
of May, retaliation for the sufferings of American prisoners,
and other reasons of policy and prudence, were assigned

for the causes of my imprisonment; but since that, having been more closely pressed for my release, and having no good reason to alledge why I should not be exchanged as well as others, they answered, for the first time, that I *might* be considered as amenable to law martial *as* a *Spy*, but graciously gave me to understand, they would not *totally* proceed to such extremities. They had still a further subterfuge. The following note was sent me a few days after the above hearing from the committee:

The committee appointed to take into consideration the application of Lieutenant Colonel Connolly, request that gentleman will inform them of his reasons for not producing and pleading his commission, at the time he was first taken, and for a considerable time afterwards.

Thursday 12 *o'clock.*

It appears really astonishing, to think that a body of men could suffer such a note to escape them, when my papers had several times, and my commission among the rest, been examined; but the fact was, they wanted to publish something to the world, that should, in my case, have at least the semblance and plausibility of justice. However, I made them so cautious an answer, that they were obliged to drop this plea, and once again take refuge under the Spy. Accordingly, in about two months after this committee first gave me a hearing, and pretended to examine into the true state of the business, the following report and resolve of Congress were published:

CONGRESS, Nov. 12, 1778.

The committee, to whom was referred a letter from John Beatty, Commissary of Prisoners, dated September 15th, 1778, together with two letters from Joshua Loring, Esq.; of the 1st of September and 28th of October, and sundry letters from John Connolly, report the following state of facts:

That Doctor John Connolly (now stiling himself Lieutenant-Colonel in the British service) was, in the latter end of November, 1775, apprehended in Frederick county, in Maryland, in company with a certain Allen Cameron, and John Smyth, by the Committee of Inspection of that county. That at the time he was taken, he was not in arms, or at the head of any party of men in arms, but was clandestinely making his way to Detroit, in order to join, give intelligence to, and otherwise aid the garrison at that place, as appears by his own intercepted letters of the 16th of December, 1775.

That a number of officers in the British service, who were made prisoners, long after the said John Connolly was apprehended, have been exchanged in course; and no demand has been made (till within these few months past) by any British General, for the release or exchange of the officer last-mentioned.

With respect to the treatment of the said Lieutenant-Colonel Connolly, the Committee report:

That at the time when he was first apprehended, he was confined under guard, by the Committee of Inspection in the town of Frederick, in an apartment separate from his associates, without any circumstance to aggravate his captivity, except the being debarred the use of pen, ink, and paper: That, notwithstanding this restraint, he contrived to write several letters of intelligence to the British officers commanding at the posts of Detroit and Kuskuskis, which letters were found on the person of Dr. Smyth, one of his associates, who, having escaped from the town of Frederick, was again apprehended:

That by the resolution of Congress, of the 8th of December, 1775, he was ordered to be confined in prison at Philadelphia; that being brought to that city, he was confined in the new gaol, wherein he continued till about the month of November, 1776, when he was permitted, on account of a declining state of health, to reside on his parole, at the house of his brother-in-law, on the river Susquehannah, where he continued for about two months; when, on information being given to the Council of Safety, of the State of Pennsylvania, of certain suspicious circumstances relative to him, he was remanded to his former place of confinement, in which he continued till about the spring, 1777, when he was again permitted on his parole, and the security of his brother-in-law, to return to his former place of residence on the river Susquehannah:

That during these periods of his confinement in the new gaol, he had, for the greatest part of the time, a separate apartment to himself, the privilege of walking in the yard, a person allowed to attend him in his apartment, and his own servant permitted to fetch him such necessaries as he chose to order.

That during the short period, when he had not a separate apartment, there were never more than two persons in the same room, seldom more than one, and those, some of his associates, or in consequence of his particular request:

That during these periods of time, he made two attempts to escape, in which he was detected:

That on authentic information being given to Congress, at York-Town, that the said Lieut. Col. John Connolly, was acting in a manner not consistent with the spirit of his parole, and the frontiers being threatened with a barbarous war, in which there was reason to apprehend he was designed as an instrument, he was ordered into confinement in the gaol at York-Town on the 13th of October:

That on the 17th of May, the said J. Connolly, with several others confined in said gaol, made a representation to Congress, setting forth in the strongest colouring, the hardships and cruelties which they declared they were then suffering:

That on the result of a strict enquiry, and after the gaol had been visited by Colonel Pickering, one of the members to the Board of War, it appeared, that the suggestions contained in the said representation, were scandalous and groundless; and the report of the Board of War, was, on the 23d day of May, ordered to be published:

That since the evacuation of Philadelphia, the said J. Connolly was remanded to the new gaol in that city, where (excepting the space of about fourteen days, when two persons were necessarily obliged to sleep in the same room) he has had a separate and commodious apartment of his own choice, the privilege of his own servant to attend him constantly, and to bring him whatever he may require, and the unrestrained use of a spacious yard to take the air in, during the day:

That in his letter of the 12th of October, 1778, the said J. Connolly declared, " That the common rights of humanity are denied to him," and paints his situation in such terms, as would tend to induce a belief, that the most wanton cruelties and restraints are imposed upon him :

That in consequence of a request of J. Connolly, to be heard in person by Committee of Congress, this Committee have complied with this request, when he declared, in presence of your Committee, " that, excepting the restraint of his person, under the limits above-mentioned, which, however indulgent they might appear, he conceived unfavourable to his state of health, he experienced every other relief which could be extended to a person in confinement :"

That Joshua Loring, Esq; British Commissary of prisoners, in his letter to Mr. Beatty of the first of September, 1778, threatens to retaliate on an American prisoner at war, of equal rank with Lieutenant Colonel Connolly, for the sufferings which, it is pretended that officer endures."

Whereupon, Resolved, That Lieutenant Colonel John Connolly, cannot of right, claim to be considered and treated as a prisoner of war; but that he was, at the time he was apprehended, and still is, *amenable to the law martial, as a spy and emissary from the British army:* . . . that the repeated representations made by Lieut. Col. John Connolly, of the grievances he undergoes, are not founded on facts: . . . That General Washington be directed to transmit the foregoing resolutions and state of facts, to the Commander in Chief of his Britanic Majesty's forces in New-York; and to inform the said officer, that if, under the pretext of retaliating for the pretended sufferings of a person, who, by the law of nations, has no right to be considered as a prisoner of war, any American officer, entitled to be con-

sidered and treated as a prisoner of war, shall undergo any
extraordinary restraints or sufferings, Congress are determined to retaliate on the person of an officer of the first
rank in their possession, for every species of hardship or
restraint on such account inflicted.

Extract from the minutes,

CHARLES THOMPSON, *Secretary.*

Though the inconsistencies of this paper are, I hope,
evident from the facts before related, yet as they may not
strike a mind less interested with the same force, I beg to
be indulged while I point out a few of them.

They make it one of my crimes, that although I was debarred the use of pen, ink, and paper, I, notwithstanding,
contrived to write several letters of intelligence to British
officers.   This is ridiculous; for, certainly, if I had the
means, it was as much my duty to aid my Sovereign when
in prison, as when at liberty, I not having given, by parole,
any promise to the contrary.

Another of my sins is, that I made two attempts to
escape!

Sometimes they call me Doctor, sometimes Lieutenant-
Colonel, and sometimes John Connolly; but when they
speak of the *lex talionis*, they threaten to retaliate on the
person of an officer of the *first rank* in their possession.

Another part of their report is contrary to truth: after
the evacuation of Philadelphia, they say I was *remanded* back
to the new gaol in that city.   The fact is as before related;
I was going from York-Town to Elizabeth-Town, on my
parole, to be exchanged, and was stopped at Philadelphia;
but it did not suit their purpose to state it in this light.

They say no demand has been made, till within these few
months past, by any British General for my release, or exchange.   This is an equivocation which must be explained
in justice to Sir William Howe.   I had come down to Philadelphia, in consequence of a *general* exchange of prisoners;
which, previous thereto, could never be settled, owing to
the impediments inseparable from a state of warfare in a

rebellion. It could not, therefore, militate against that commander, as inattentive to the condition of a loyal American. I must likewise acknowledge, with the warmest gratitude, the zeal with which Sir Henry Clinton insisted upon my release, although this equitable and generous interference had nearly effected my destruction; for finding themselves, when they made the above resolve, in possession of General Phillips, and other officers of rank, the Congress was determined to keep me; and the threat of retaliation, however disguised, was palpably levelled at the last-mentioned General, and was, in fact, a plain declaration to Sir Henry Clinton, that I *should not then be exchanged.*

I owe, indeed, every obligation to Sir Henry's attention; for when the report, which the emissaries of Congress had propagated that I was not commissioned, reached the British lines; to obviate immediately that pretence, and all undue advantages that might be taken, had my commission been lost by any accident, or out of my power to produce, he instantly caused the following certificate to be transmitted to Philadelphia:

INSPECTOR GENERAL'S OFFICE, New York,
November 27, 1778.

This is to certify, that John Connolly, Esq; was appointed Lieutenant-Colonel in his Majesty's service, by his Excellency Lord Dunmore; and said Lieutenant-Colonel Connolly is now confined in prison by the enemy, in Philadelphia; and I further certify, that I have received Lieutenant-Colonel Connolly's full subsistence, up to the 25th December, 1778, by order of his Excellency Sir Henry Clinton, Commander in Chief of his Majesty's forces in North America.

H. ROOK,
D. I. G. P. forces.

(*Copy from the original.*)

I shall forbear to reason upon, or take any further notice of that part of their report, where they endeavour to shew I had not endured any peculiar hardships in my imprisonment, or of their treating me as a spy in their resolve, having before spoken to those points, but shall proceed with my narrative.

Some time after this, Doctor Berkenhout arrived at Philadelphia from New York, and was imprisoned on some suspicions, by which accident I became acquainted with that Gentleman, and much conversation passed between us concerning the most probable means of my obtaining my liberty. Shortly after he was delivered from his confinement, an order of Congress, under the signature of their Secretary, came to the keeper to lock me up in my room (I having then the privilege of walking in the gaol yard), place a centinel at my door, and allow no person whatever to converse with me. The complexion of the times, the formality of the order, coming immediately too from Congress, and the strictness with which it was enforced, gave me reason to believe that the last tragic act was now to take place, and that I should be released from my sufferings by execution; and in such a state were both my mind and body, that this imagination gave far more pleasure than pain. I remained in this suspense for six weeks, when my door was again thrown open, and I was allowed to walk in the yard.

It afterwards appeared, that Mr. Silas Deane, in his defence of his public transactions while Ambassador to the Court of France, had affirmed, he had discovered, by means of his emissaries at New York, that Dr. Berkenhout had made a proposition to the British General, to suspend all exchange of American officers till I was admitted to be exchanged, and that I was then to be sent to the northward, to carry on a predatory war, whence he asserted, he had saved the inhabitants of the United States from the horrors of Indian hostilities. This, absurd as it was, and calculated on private views only, was the cause of my above close confinement.

Soon afterwards I was suddenly attacked by a cholera morbus, and continued in so languishing a state, that in the beginning of April, 1779, a certificate of my infirmities was signed by two of the most eminent physicians in Philadelphia, and sent by them to Congress, wherein they declared, that unless I was allowed the open air, I must fall a victim to imprisonment, on which I was allowed to ride four hours a day, within the limits of about two miles, but on my parole, obliged to return every night to confinement. It was intimated likewise, I should soon be sent to Reading and exchanged; but even the indulgence of riding in the open air, was presently prohibited, and I again shut up in prison.

Thus I continued till the 17th of November, at which time, in consequence of the return of General Sullivan, from his expedition against Colonel Butler and the Indian auxiliaries, in which he was supposed to have greatly intimidated those people; and as it was evident, that my health was in a manner irreparably impaired, and the future of the war more favourable to Congress, they came to the following resolve :

In Congress.

Read a report from the Board of War.

Whereupon resolved,

That the Commissary-General of prisoners be authorized to exchange Lieutenant-Colonel John Connolly, for any Lieutenant-Colonel in the service of the United States, now a prisoner with the enemy.

By order of Congress,

Signed

CHARLES THOMPSON, *Secretary.*

I was quickly after sent to German Town on parole, and on the 4th of July, 1780, allowed to go to New-York on the following conditions :

Philadelphia.

His Excellency General Washington having granted me permission to repair to the City of New-York on parole, for the purpose of negociating my exchange for that of Lieutenant-Colonel Ramsay, I do promise, on my word of honour and faith as a gentleman, that I will pass from here on the direct road to the said City of New-York, by the way of Elizabeth Town, and that I will return to captivity at the expiration of one month from this day, unless within that time the above-mentioned exchange is effected.

I do, in like manner, pledge my word and sacred honour, that I will not, directly nor indirectly, say or do any thing injurious to the United States of America, or the armies thereof; but that I will in all things conduct myself as a prisoner of war ought and should do, under the indulgence granted me.

It is worthy of remark, that, in the resolve, Congress authorized me to be exchanged for *any* Lieutenant-Colonel in the service of the United States; but in the strange parole, which they obliged me to give, they insist upon a particular person, a favourite Colonel. However, that all necessity of my return to Philadelphia might be totally superseded, the Commander in Chief allowed Colonel Ramsay to set off on his parole immediately, and the final adjustment of the matter was deferred till the 25th of October, 1780, at which time, after suffering what I have related, in an imprisonment of almost five years, I congratulated myself on a restoration to liberty.

I was no sooner free, than I was highly solicitous to be employed in the mode most likely to render service. I had observed that Lord Cornwallis, now advancing from the southward, was often retarded by the temporary junction of the Militia with the Congressional troops. I knew the country, the capacity and genius of these men, and the necessity of obliging them to attend to desultory operations in their rear, to facilitate his Lordship's gallant endeavours. I, therefore, submitted a plan to the consideration of Sir Henry Clinton, wherein I proposed attacking some out-posts on the frontiers of the Middle Colonies, to possess myself of Pittsburgh, fortify the passes of the Allegheney Mountains, and with Provincial troops, and Indian auxiliaries, act as emergencies might require. His Excellency was pleased to approve of this measure; but as the season was too far advanced to arrive in proper time on the proposed field of action, by the circuitous route of the river St. Lawrence and the lakes, it was laid aside.

In the month of April, 1781, I found myself very ill; but as his Excellency intimated early in June a wish that I should join the army under Lord Cornwallis, though I knew the danger of the hot climates to my constitution at that time, I did not suffer myself to hesitate a moment, but obeyed. I had hope, too, of here effecting another purpose; about which I was extremely anxious. I was without a regiment, and was endeavouring to raise one at New-York; but as the recruiting there went on very slowly, I flattered myself I might be enabled to compleat my corps to the southward; and before my departure, his Excellency was pleased to confirm my rank as Lieutenant Colonel in the Provincial line.

Having joined Lord Cornwallis, and following him to York-Town, an enemy's fleet being daily expected on the coast, his Lordship appointed me to the command of the Virginia and North Carolina Loyalists, with a detachment of the York Volunteers. I was directed to move down to Back River, to protect the inhabitants of the Peninsula, lying between the Chesapeak-Bay and James River, who were exposed to the ravages of armed boats from the eastern shore of Virginia. I had not marched above five miles on this expedition, before I was obliged to halt, being informed the French fleet had arrived, and that two seventy-four gun ships were actually at the entrance of York-River. I was, therefore, ordered to return to the vicinity of York-Town.

The men had underwent excessive fatigue in an inclement climate; had been obliged to drink noxiou water; the horses in the legionary camp were lying dead in numbers; the negroes that followed the army could hardly be buried fast enough; and the putrescent effluvia, that consequently followed, made the air too unwholesome for the small remains of vigour in my constitution to resist its effects. Lying in the field brought on a dysentery; I was obliged to go into sick quarters; and the disorder turned to a debilitating diarrhœa, that reduced me to almost the last extremity. Remaining in the town was certain death; and the only remedy was a change of air. I had been invited by some loyal gentlemen to their houses, and as the inhabitants of the Peninsula had either been admitted to parole, or had taken the oath of allegiance, there seemed little danger in accepting the invitation; yet, as it was possible, though, as I supposed, very improbable, I might again fall into the hands of the enemy, desperate as my state of health then certainly was, I would not venture into the country till I had first informed Lord Cornwallis of my wishes, and obtained leave; which his Lordship, as humane as he is brave, instantly granted by the following note:

HEAD-QUARTERS, 21st Sept. 1781.

SIR,

I am directed by Lord Cornwallis to inform you, that he most readily consents to your going to the country, or taking any other step that you think will contribute to the establishment of your health; his Lordship wishes you a speedy and perfect recovery; and I am with great regard,

Sir,
your most obedient
most humble Servant,
A. Ross, *Aid du Camp.*

LT. COL. CONNOLLY.

Incapable of riding on horseback, I set out in a small sulkey, attended by two servants; and on the road, met the gentleman to whose house I was going, who informed me there was no danger; and perceiving me to be very weak and exhausted, went with me to a contiguous gentleman's house, and introduced me to the family, advising me to repose till the sun declined, by which time he would return from York-Town, whither he was going, and accompany me home. My friend not returning so soon as I expected, I set forward without him, but had not proceeded far before three men, with fixed bayonets, rushed out of a thicket and made me and one of my servants prisoners.

They drove my carriage into a forest of pines, and detained me till night for fear of a rescue, and then, by secret roads, conducted me to a place called New-Port-News, where I first learnt that General Washington was arrived at Williamsburgh, before whom, they insisted I must be taken, having no respect for my illness, nor any conception of admitting a prisoner, in such a predicament, to his parole. It perhaps, was happy for me, that they did not; for the air, or exercise, or both, had such an effect upon me, that when I was put to bed, I slept upwards of three hours; a refreshment to which I had been long a stranger. In fact, I have reason to believe, that though the misfortune of captivity seemed to haunt me, yet, in this instance it saved my life.

From hence I was embarqued in a whale boat, and put on board a French ship Armée en Flute, when I had the good fortune to meet with Admiral Barras, with the Artillery officers of the French army, who treated me with all the tenderness and humanity, which the feelings and politeness of gentlemen could dictate. The next day I was sent on shore to General Lincoln, who behaved to me with every respect, sent one of his Aids to accompany me, and very obligingly furnished me with his own horse, as he was remarkably gentle and safe and no carriage to be had, to carry me to General Washington.

I was now to see a man with whom I had formerly been upon a footing of intimacy, I may say of friendship. Politics might induce us to meet like enemies in the field, but should not have made us personally so. I had small time for reflection; we met him on horseback coming to view the camp. I can only say the friendly sentiments he once publicly professed for me, no longer existed. He ordered me to be conducted to the Marquis de la Fayette's quarters.

From the Marquis I received every civility and attention; and on account of my health, was entertained by him for three days, when being solicitous to avoid giving trouble, I was sent on parole by General Washington's orders, about sixty miles back into the country. Here I remained till I heard of the catastrophe at York-Town, and that the British officers were generally allowed to go into New-York. I thereupon wrote to the American Commissary General for passports, but could obtain no satisfactory answer. I applied to General Washington, and was equally disappointed. Being left alone, as it were, in an enemy's country, and no authority capable of granting my request remaining, except the Govenor's of Virginia, to him I had recourse. From this gentleman, I obtained permission to go to Philadelphia, on receiving a written assurance from me, of submitting myself there to those who had the supreme direction of prisoners. I did not reach this city till the 12th of December, when I applied to the Secretary of War, for leave to proceed to New-York, but soon found I had unexpected difficulties to encounter. I was detained at a public house above a fortnight, and then committed to prison by the following warrant, under the Seal of the Common Wealth, issued by the Executive Council, and signed by the President, a copy of which I demanded from the gaoler.

You are hereby authorized and directed to receive into your custody, a certain John Connolly, an officer in the British service, charged with having broke his parole, given in the State of Virginia, and him safely keep until he be delivered in due course of law.

Given under my hand and seal, in the Council Chamber, this twenty eighth of December, Anno Domini, 1782.

W. MOORE, *President.*

To the keeper of the gaol of the city
    and county of Philadelphia.

The above is a true copy of the original remaining in my hand.

JOHN REYNOLDS, *Gaoler.*

The pretence of a breach of parole was preposterous, and to be delivered from confinement for such an offence, by due course of law, was more so. I wrote to General Washington on the occasion, but soon discovered he did not intend I should have left Virginia, and appeared determined, at first, that I should return. To this I could not voluntarily accede, and I remained in prison till the 1st of March; when, by the interposition of friends, I was at length permitted to go to New-York, provided I went from thence to Europe, where (at New-York) I arrived on the 11th of the same month.

I must here take notice, that the raising of my intended regiment became no longer practicable, as the officers whom I had warranted for that service, with the recruits raised in Virginia, had shared a common fate with the army at York-Town; and those that remained at New-York, as soon as the war became merely defensive, were drafted into another corps.

When the fleet sailed, Sir Guy Carleton gave me permission to come to England, for the recovery of my health, where I yet continue to receive my subsistence, as Lieutenant-Colonel in the Provincial service, as will appear by the annexed letter from the Secretary of State to his Excellency Sir Guy Carleton.

WHITEHALL, Feb. 24, 1783.

SIR,

Having laid before the king a letter from Lieutenant-Colonel Delancey, Adjutant-General of the forces under your command, to Lieutenant-Colonel Connolly, acquainting him that some difficulties have arisen with regard to the propriety of issuing his pay in North-America, on account of his absence upon leave. I am, in obedience to his Majesty's commands, to acquaint you, that he is pleased to approve of your causing the pay due to Lieutenant Connolly to be

issued to him, and of its being continued, from time to
time, during his absence on leave.

> I am, Sir,
> Your most obedient,
> humble servant,
> J. TOWNSHEND.

(Signed)
SIR GUY CARLETON, K. B.

It is a duty incumbent on me to show, that the truth of
the foregoing narrative need not rest solely on my assertions, the following papers are authentic testimonials of its
veracity:

' I hereby certify, that Major John Connolly was appointed
by me to the command of the militia of West Augusta
County, in his Majesty's colony of Virginia; and that he
exerted himself as a faithful officer, in the discharge of that
duty, until the commencement of the rebellion, when the
good of the King's service, and my own personal security,
obliging me to withdraw from the seat of government, I
authorized Major Connolly to adjust all differences with the
adjacent Indian tribes, and to incline them towards his
Majesty's interest.   This service appeard to me to have been
well performed, from the belts and speeches transmitted by
their Chiefs through him to me, notwithstanding that Commissioners from the Assembly (at that time resolved into an
illegal convention), attended the treaty at Pittsburgh, in
order to influence them to assist in their meditated opposition, to the constitutional authority of this kingdom.

Upon the performance of this service, in conformity to
my direction, the troops under the command of Major Connolly at Fort Pitt, were discharged agreeable to the provision made by the Act of Assembly; and he repaired to
me, through much difficulty, with a zeal and alacrity that
bespoke the firmest loyalty.   I immediately dispatched
Major Connolly to Boston, informing General Gage of the
situation of the colony at that period; and as Major Connolly had a formidable interest in the frontiers, I proposed

his raising a body of men for his Majesty's service there, and in the contiguous parts of Quebec government, and to command an expedition, so as to co-operate with me, for the reduction of the King's enemies, for which purpose he was invested with a commission of Lieutenant-Colonel Commandant, bearing date the 5th of November, 1775, with full powers to act as emergencies might require. In the execution of this duty, Lieutenant-Colonel Connolly was unfortunately made a prisoner, and continued as such, under the immediate direction of Congress, near five years, suffering a constant state of confinement. I further certify, that Lieutenant-Colonel Connolly, from his loyalty and attachment to government, forfeited a very considerable sum of money due to him from the Assembly of Virginia, for his public services as an officer; and that his estate was also confiscated; four thousand acres of his landed property having been patented by me, whilst I had the honour to preside as his Majesty's representative in Virginia.'

Given under my hand the 25th day of October, 1782.
(Signed)   DUNMORE.

' I certify, that Lieutenant-Colonel Connolly, came from his Excellency the Earl of Dunmore to Boston, in the year 1775, and laid before me certain propositions for the suppression of his Majesty's enemies in the colony of Virginia; to promote which, I gave orders to a detachment of the King's troops, then in the Illinois, to receive the directions of Lord Dunmore; and I further certify, that in the execution of this duty, it was reported to me, that Lieutenant-Colonel Connolly was made a prisoner by the enemy, and that from every appearance, he manifested the greatest loyalty and attachment to the constitutional authority of government.'

Given under my hand, this 30th day of October, 1782.
(Signed)   THOMAS GAGE.

What I have said in this recapitulation will meet, I hope, on every hand, with a candid construction. It is a cutting reflection to find, on looking it through, that it is a tale of

sickness and misfortunes, instead of a history of glorious
actions and essential services; but the assigned causes are
surely a sufficient apology. The contemplative and humane
must commiserate the infirmities of nature, whilst the mag-
nanimous and enterprizing must dread similar impediments
in the pursuit of glory. In my own vindication I have been
obliged to speak of persons and things as they were, but I
hope this has been done without exaggeration or malignity.
I wish not to revive animosities had I the power, nor to
complain of men who, whatever were their motives then
for inflicting severities upon me in particular, are never
likely to have the same cause, or the same opportunity.
They, doubtless, thought themselves acting virtuously, and
would plead the love of their country, in extenuation of
errors: I must do the same, with this addition, my virtues,
in their eyes, became my crimes; let not my misfortunes,
in the eye of government, become my faults. I shall conclude, with a few reflections on the nature of the Provincial
service, before and during the Civil Wars, and of what I
deem my consequent and reasonable claims on this country.

Before the dismemberment of the British empire, the
provincial officer in North America knew, with precision,
upon what footing he took the field, to co-operate with
British troops, to prevent incursion, or effect conquest. His
rank was determined by the King, and wherever he acted
in conjunction with his fellow-subjects of this country, either
within his own province, or in another colony, every difficulty
was obviated. He was considered as the junior officer: this
was evidently an equitable and a sufficiently honourable
mark of Royal favour. The loyalty that induced him to
espouse the quarrels of Britain in America, promoted, likewise, the security of his own property, and restored the
blessings of peace and affluence to himself, his friends, and
countrymen. Few reflected that it was as British colonists
they were involved in the wars of Britain, or that a separate
system of government could withhold them from seconding
the interest of the parent state. As Englishmen they felt,
and as Englishmen they were ready to act; but as the entire

professional soldier, select from the body of his fellow-subjects, was but of a temporary nature, and the return of peace replaced him in his former happy station, it would have been unjust to have expected the permanent rank and emoluments of him, who devoted himself wholly to the possession of the sword. It is the immunities of a member of this empire, founded upon the broad basis of equity and justice, that must give efficacy to reasonable pretensions.

In former wars, when American subjects acted in conformity to the orders of their sovereign, and were commissioned by the royal representative to military command, the pecuniary advantages annexed to the respective stations in which they appeared, arose from the acts of general assembly of the governments wherein they resided; and this provision more ample, or circumscribed, depended upon the temper or generosity of the different legislatures. The late unfortunate dispute, wherein not only the prerogative of the King, but the supremacy of the Parliament of his Kingdom, was the litigated cause between Britain and her colonies, and in the maintenance of which, the American loyalist who attempted to support this system as constitutional, took an active part, changed totally the nature of his political connexions. Cut off from his former dependance by the issue of the war, excluded from the privileges of the community to which he belonged, and deprived of his property as a mark of its displeasure and disapprobation of his conduct, to whom can he apply for retribution, but to that power which has been the source of his misfortunes? Or how can he be more honourably or equitably treated in the society to which he is now attached, than by a provision in that line by which he became a sufferer. Congress have asserted, that we were destined by Britain to be hewers of wood, and drawers of water. The time is now arrived, when ample opportunity is allowed to contradict this ungenerous aspersion, and full scope given to the exercise of that generosity of disposition and liberality of sentiment, for which I hope this nation will forever appear as the fairest candidate. The peculiarity of my case is without parallel, and my pretensions, if as successful as just can afford no precedent.   The troops to be raised under my orders, both from Canada and Virginia, must illustrate the conditions upon which I entered the service, and plainly shew that my intended operations were not merely Colonial, as an inhabitant of Virginia, but that from the St Lawrence to the Mississippi, I was equally ready to obey the royal mandate.   Commissioned as Lieutenant-Colonel, unconditionally by the King's representative, at the commencement of the rebellion, and taken in the execution of my duty as a faithful servant of the Crown, held in captivity five years by the enemy, to prevent the efforts of my capacity, to disregard my claim, as the consequence of such misfortunes, my sufferings, my zeal, and loyalty, must then operate as my greatest faults; and what I ever flattered myself, must argue in my favour, would unexpectly complete the measure of my disappointment from captivity.

Upon my releasement, as the war was changed from an offensive to defensive one, in the Northern Colonies, and the prospect of raising a corps in circumscribed limits where I had no particular interest, but faint and unpromising, the Commander in Chief, sensible of the hardness of my case, was pleased to confirm my rank in the provincial line.   And I must beg leave to offer my being fully subsisted as Lieut. Col. and which I yet continue to receive, as a corroborating proof of my merits, and the propriety of my present requisition.

In fact, feeling as I do, the cause of exultation the disappointment would afford my political enemies, and the oblique implied reflection upon my character, from a treatment less distinguishing than my loyal countrymen of the same rank, I must beg leave to insinuate, that I can receive no adequate recompence through any other channel.   A compensation for my loss of estate is, in that case, all I require; and I shall endeavour to support this unmerited adversity, with that conscious dignity of mind, which I hope will never forsake me, and in a manner the least exceptionable.   JOHN CONNOLLY.

www.ingramcontent.com/pod-product-compliance
Lightning Source LLC
Chambersburg PA
CBHW021515090426
42739CB00007B/621